I0017434

This page is intentionally left blank

Table of content

Chapter 1: Introduction to Python   **5**
    1.1. Why Python?   5
    1.2. Scope of this Book   5
    1.3. History of Python   6
    1.4. Setting up a Python development environment   7
    1.5. Basic concepts of programming   7
    1.6. Introduction to the Python syntax   8

Chapter 2: Modules and libraries   **9**
    2.1. Modules   9
    2.2. Libraries   10

Chapter 3: Variables   **11**
    3.1. What are Variables?   11
    3.2. Variable types   11
    3.3. Strings   12
        3.3.1. What are Strings?   12
        3.3.2. Concatenation   14
        3.3.3. Replacement   14
        3.3.4. Case conversion   14
        3.3.5. Whitespace removal   15
        3.3.6. Splitting   15
        3.3.7. Searching   15
        3.3.8. Formatting   16
    3.4. Booleans   16
        3.4.1. Overview   16
        3.4.2. Comparison operation   16
    3.5. Numbers   17
        3.5.1. Overview   17
        3.5.2. int, float, complex   18
        3.5.3. Built-in functions   18
        3.5.4. Mathematics   19
    3.6. Variable conversion   19
    3.7. Users inputs   20
    3.8. Pro-Trip: Good practices for Variables   20

Chapter 4: Operators   **22**
    4.1. Arithmetic operators   22
    4.2. Assignment operators   22
    4.3. Comparison operators   24
    4.4. Logical operators   25
    4.5. Identity operators   27

4.6. Membership operators 28

4.7. Bitwise operators 29

Chapter 5: Data types **31**

5.1. Lists 31

    5.1.1. What are Lists? 31

    5.1.2. Access elements 31

    5.1.3. Change or add values 33

    5.1.4. Pro Tips: When to use Lists 33

5.2. Tuples 34

    5.2.1. What are Tuples? 34

    5.2.2. Access elements 35

    5.2.3. Mixing types 35

    5.2.4. Tuple Slicing 35

    5.2.5. Tuple Unpacking 36

    5.2.6. Tuple Methods and Functions 36

    5.2.7. Pro Tips: When to use Tuples 37

5.3. Dictionaries 37

    5.3.1. What are Dictionaries? 37

    5.3.2. Accessing Dictionary Items 38

    5.3.3. Add / Delete / Update key-value pairs 38

    5.3.4. List all keys 39

    5.3.5. Dictionaries built-in methods 40

    5.3.6. Pro-Tips: When to use Dictionaries 41

Chapter 6: Control structures **43**

6.1. if / elif / else statements 43

6.2. for loops 44

    6.2.1. What are for loops? 44

    6.2.2. Iterating over a range of numbers 45

    6.2.3. Iterating over a list 45

    6.2.4. Iterating over a string 46

    6.2.5. Using the enumerate function 46

    6.2.6. Using the zip function 46

    6.2.7. The for-else loop 47

    6.2.8. Conclusion 47

6.3. while loops 47

    6.3.1. What are while loops? 47

    6.3.2. Using the break keyword 48

    6.3.3. Using the continue keyword 49

    6.3.4. The while-else loop 49

    6.3.5. The infinite loop 50

    6.3.6. Conclusion 50

Chapter 7: Functions **51**

7.1. Defining and calling functions 51

7.1.1. What is a function? 51
7.1.2. Defining a function 51
7.1.3. Calling a function 51
7.2. Parameters and arguments 52
7.2.1. Overview 52
7.2.2. Default parameter values 52
7.2.3. Variable length arguments 53
7.3. Return values 53
7.4. Variable scope 54

Chapter 8: File input and output **56**
8.1. Overview 56
8.2. Working with Files 56
8.2.1. Reading from a File 56
8.2.2. Writing to a File 57
8.2.3. Pro-Tips: All modes for the open() function 57
8.3. Working with JSON files 58
8.3.1. Overview 58
8.3.2. Creating a JSON test file 58
8.3.3. Reading JSON Data 59
8.3.4. Writing JSON Data 60
8.3.5. Pro-Tips: Python Object / JSON String conversion 60

Chapter 9: Python projects for beginners **61**
9.1. Overview 61
9.2. Building a Celsius-Fahrenheit Converter 61
9.2.1. Goals 61
9.2.2. Instructions 62
9.2.3. Source code 62
9.2.4. Demonstration 63
9.3. Building a simple Calculator 63
9.3.1. Goals 63
9.3.2. Instructions 64
9.3.3. Source code 65
9.3.4. Demonstration 66
9.4. Building a simple Game 66
9.4.1. Goals 66
9.4.2. Instructions 66
9.4.3. Source code 67
9.4.4. Demonstration 68
9.5. Building a Password Generator 69
9.5.1. Goals 69
9.5.2. Instructions 69
9.5.3. Source code 70
9.5.4. Demonstration 71

9.6. Building a TO-DO List   71
    9.6.1. Goals   71
    9.6.2. Instructions   72
    9.6.3. Source code   72
    9.6.4. Demonstration   73
9.7. Building a Web Scraper   75
    9.7.1. Goals   75
    9.7.2. Instructions   75
    9.7.3. Source code   76
    9.7.4. Demonstration   77
9.8. Building a Tic-Tac-Toe Game   77
    9.8.1. Goals   77
    9.8.2. Instructions   78
    9.8.3. Source code   78
    9.8.4. Demonstration   80
9.9. Building a Weather Forecast App (API)   81
    9.9.1. Goals   81
    9.9.2. Instructions   81
    9.9.3. Source code   82
    9.9.4. Demonstration   84

Chapter 10: Conclusion   **85**
10.1. Recap of key Python concepts   85
10.2. Next steps for learning Python   85

Chapter 1: Introduction to Python

1.1. Why Python?

Python is a popular programming language that is widely used in a variety of applications, including web development, scientific computing, data analysis, and artificial intelligence. It is known for its simplicity, readability, and flexibility, which make it a great language for beginners to learn.

In summary:

- Python is a **popular** and **widely-used** programming language that is used in a variety of applications, including web development, scientific computing, data analysis, and artificial intelligence.
- Python is known for its **simplicity**, **readability**, and **flexibility**, which make it a great language for beginners to learn. It has a concise and intuitive syntax, and there are many resources and tutorials available to help you get started.
- Python is a **high-level** language, which means that it abstracts away many of the details of how a computer works. This makes it easier to focus on solving problems and creating programs, rather than worrying about low-level details like memory management and data types.
- Python has a large and active **community** of developers, which means that there is a wealth of knowledge and resources available online. There are also many third-party libraries and frameworks that you can use to extend the capabilities of Python and build powerful applications.
- Python is a **versatile** language that is used in many different fields, including finance, education, research, and more. This means that you can use Python to build a wide range of applications and projects, and there are many **career** opportunities available for Python developers.

1.2. Scope of this Book

This book is designed to provide a comprehensive introduction to the Python programming language, with a focus on the most recent version, **Python 3**. Throughout the book, you will learn the fundamental concepts and syntax of Python, as well as how to apply these concepts to real-world projects.

We will cover a range of topics including:

- Programming basics

- Python syntax
- Variables
- Operators
- Data types
- Control structures
- Functions and modules
- Reading and writing files
- Handling data structures (including JSON manipulation)

Additionally, the book features **eight complete Python projects** (source codes are available on GitHub) to help you practice and reinforce your understanding of the material.

Overall, this book is an excellent resource for anyone looking to learn Python from the ground up, whether you are a beginner programmer or an experienced developer looking to expand your skill set.

1.3. History of Python

Python was created by **Guido van Rossum** in the late **1980s**. Van Rossum was working on a project at the National Research Institute for Mathematics and Computer Science in the Netherlands (CWI) at the time, and he needed a language that was easy to use and had a simple syntax. Python was first released in **1991**, and it has undergone many changes and improvements since then.

Python was named after the British comedy group Monty Python, and it was initially intended to be a hobby project. However, it quickly gained popularity and became a full-time project for van Rossum.

Python has a large and active community of developers who contribute to the language and its ecosystem. There are also many organizations and companies that use Python and support its development.

Python has been widely adopted in a variety of fields, including web development, scientific computing, data analysis, and artificial intelligence. It is used by many large organizations, including Google, NASA, and the New York Stock Exchange.

Over the years, Python has become **one of the most popular programming languages in the world**, with a large and active community of developers. It is widely used in many different fields, including web development, data analysis, scientific computing, and artificial intelligence.

1.4. Setting up a Python development environment

Before you can start programming in Python, you will need to set up a development environment on your computer. This involves installing a Python interpreter, which is a program that runs your Python code, and a **text editor** or **integrated development environment (IDE)**, which is a program that you will use to write and edit your code.

There are many different options for setting up a Python development environment, depending on your operating system and preferences. Some popular options include:

- Using the Python **interpreter** that comes pre-installed on most Unix-based systems
- Installing a **standalone Python interpreter**, such as the official Python distribution from python.org
- Using a pre-configured Python development environment, such as **Anaconda** or **PyCharm**

Once you have set up your development environment, you are ready to start writing and running your first Python program!

1.5. Basic concepts of programming

Before diving into the specifics of the Python language, it is important to understand some basic concepts that are common to all programming languages.

These include:

- **Variables**: A variable is a named storage location in a computer's memory that can hold a value. In Python, you can create a variable by assigning a value to it using the assignment operator (=). For example: **x = 5** creates a variable x and assigns it the value 5.
- **Data types**: Different types of data, such as numbers, strings, and lists, have different properties and can be used in different ways. Python has a number of built-in data types, including integers, floating-point numbers, strings, and lists.
- **Operators**: Operators are special symbols that perform operations on variables or values. Python has a variety of operators, including arithmetic operators (e.g., +, -, *, /), comparison operators (e.g., ==, !=, >, <), and logical operators (e.g., and, or, not).
- **Control structures**: Control structures are used to control the flow of a program. Python has several control structures, including if statements, for loops, and while loops, that allow you to execute different blocks of code depending on certain conditions or to repeat a block of code multiple times.

We will discuss each of these concepts and provide examples.

1.6.   Introduction to the Python syntax

The syntax of a programming language is the set of rules that govern the structure and organization of the code. Python has a simple and easy-to-learn syntax, which makes it a popular choice for beginners.

Some of the key features of the Python syntax include:

- **Indentation**: In Python, indentation is used to denote blocks of code. This means that the indentation level of a line of code determines how it is grouped with other lines of code. For example, a block of code that is indented one level is considered to be a child of the block of code that it is indented under.
- **Line breaks**: In Python, a line break indicates the end of a statement. This means that you can spread a statement over multiple lines by using a line break, as long as you indent the subsequent lines correctly.
- **Comments**: Comments are lines of code that are ignored by the interpreter and are used to add notes or documentation to your code. In Python, you can create a comment by starting a line with the # symbol.

That's it for the first chapter! I hope this gives you a good foundation for learning Python.

Chapter 2: Modules and libraries

2.1. Modules

A module is a file containing Python code that can be imported into other Python scripts or programs. Modules can define functions, classes, and variables, and they can be used to organize and reuse code.

Python comes with a large number of built-in modules, which provide a wide range of functions and capabilities. For example, the **math** module provides mathematical functions like **sin**, **cos**, and **sqrt**, and the **random** module provides functions for generating random numbers.

You can import a module into your Python script or program using the **import** statement. For example, to use the math module, you would write "**import math**" at the top of your script. You can then use the functions and variables defined in the module by prefixing them with the module name, like this: **math.sin(x)** or **math.pi**.

For example, you can import this **math** module into your script by using the import statement:

```
import math

x = math.sin(math.pi / 2)  # x = 1.0
y = math.cos(0)  # y = 1.0
z = math.sqrt(2)  # z = 1.4142
```

In this example, the **math** module is imported and its functions are used to calculate the sine, cosine, and square root of various values.

You can also import specific functions from a module using the from keyword:

```
from math import sin, cos

x = sin(math.pi / 2)  # x = 1.0
y = cos(0)  # y = 1.0
```

In this case, only the **sin** and **cos** functions are imported from the math module, so you don't need to specify the **math** prefix when using them.

2.2. Libraries

In addition to the built-in modules, there are many third-party modules and libraries available that you can use to extend the capabilities of Python. These libraries are often distributed as package files that can be installed using the **pip** or **conda** package managers.

Some popular third-party libraries for Python include **NumPy** and **SciPy** for scientific computing, **Pandas** for data manipulation and analysis, and **Matplotlib** for data visualization. There are also many frameworks available for web development, machine learning, and other applications.

For example, the **numpy** library is a popular library for scientific computing that provides functions for working with arrays, matrices, and numerical operations. To use a library, you will need to install it using a package manager like pip and then import it into your script or program.

To install the **numpy** library using pip, you can use the following command:

```
pip install numpy
```

This will install the numpy library and its dependencies on your system. You can then use it in your Python scripts or programs by importing it as below:

```python
import numpy as np

a = np.array([1, 2, 3])  # Create a 1-dimensional array
b = np.array([[1, 2, 3], [4, 5, 6]])  # Create a 2-dimensional array
c = np.dot(a, b)  # Matrix multiplication
```

In this example, the **numpy** library is imported using the alias np, and its functions are used to create and manipulate arrays.

Modules and libraries are an essential part of Python programming, and they provide a way to organize, reuse, and share code.

Chapter 3: Variables

3.1.   What are Variables?

In programming, a variable is a named location in memory where a value can be stored and accessed. Variables are used to store data that can change during the execution of a program.

In Python, you can create a variable by assigning a value to it using the assignment operator (=). The name of the variable can be any combination of letters, digits, and underscores (_) as long as it does not start with a digit and is not a reserved word.

Here is an example of creating a variable and assigning a value to it:

```
x = 10
```

In this example, we create a variable named x and assign the value 10 to it. The type of the value stored in a variable is determined automatically by the interpreter based on the value assigned to it. In this case, the type of x is **int** (integer).

You can also assign a value of a different type to a variable.

For example, the following will change the value of x to a **string**:

```
x = 'hello'
```

3.2.   Variable types

In Python, the type of a variable is determined automatically based on the value assigned to it. Here are some of the basic types in Python:

- **int**: Integer type. Examples: 1, -100, 0
- **float**: Floating point type. Examples: 3.14, -2.5, 0.0
- **str**: String type. Examples: 'hello', "world", '123'
- **bool**: Boolean type. Examples: True, False

You can use the type function to check the type of a variable:

```
x = 10
print(type(x))   # Output: <class 'int'>

x = 3.14
print(type(x))   # Output: <class 'float'>

x = 'hello'
print(type(x))   # Output: <class 'str'>

x = True
print(type(x))   # Output: <class 'bool'>
```

3.3.   Strings

3.3.1.   What are Strings?

In Python, a string is a sequence of characters enclosed in quotation marks (either single or double). Strings are used to represent text and are an essential data type in Python.

Here is an example of how to create a string in Python:

```
# Create a string
s = "Hello, World!"

# You can also use single quotes to create a string
s = 'Hello, World!'

# You can even use triple quotes to create a multi-line string
s = """
Hello,
World!
"""
```

You can access individual characters in a string using indexing.

The first character has index 0, the second character has index 1, and so on.

Here is an example:

```
# Access the first character of a string
print(s[0])   # Output: "H"

# Access the third character of a string
print(s[2])   # Output: "l"
```

You can also use negative indexing to access characters from the end of the string. For example, the last character has index -1, the second to last character has index -2, and so on.

```
# Access the last character of a string
print(s[-1])  # Output: "!"

# Access the second to last character of a string
print(s[-2])  # Output: "d"
```

You can slice a string to extract a sub-string by specifying a range of indices. The syntax is **s[start:end]**, where **start** is the index of the first character to include in the slice and **end** is the index of the first character to exclude from the slice.

For example:

```
# Extract the sub-string "World" from the string "Hello, World!"
sub_string = s[7:12]
print(sub_string)  # Output: "World"
```

You can also omit the **start** or **end** index to include all characters from the beginning or end of the string, respectively.

For example:

```
# Extract all characters from the beginning of the string
sub_string = s[:5]
print(sub_string)  # Output: "Hello"

# Extract all characters from the end of the string
sub_string = s[7:]
print(sub_string)  # Output: "World!"
```

You can also use a step value to skip characters in the slice. The syntax is **s[start:end:step]**.

For example:

```
# Extract every other character from the string "Hello, World!"
sub_string = s[::2]
print(sub_string)  # Output: "HloWrd"
```

3.3.2. Concatenation

Strings are **immutable** in Python, which means that you cannot change the value of a string once it has been created. However, you can create a new string by concatenating (joining) multiple strings together using the **+ operator**.

For example:

```
# Concatenate two strings
s1 = "Hello"
s2 = ", World!"
s3 = s1 + s2
print(s3)  # Output: "Hello, World!"
```

You can also use the string method "join" to concatenate a list of strings.

For example:

```
# Concatenate a list of strings using the "join" method
s4 = "".join(["Hello", ", ", "World!"])
print(s4)  # Output: "Hello, World!"
```

3.3.3. Replacement

The **replace** method allows you to search for a sub-string within a string and replace it with another string.

For example:

```
# Replace a sub-string in a string with another string using the
"replace" method
s5 = s4.replace("World", "Python")
print(s5)  # Output: "Hello, Python!"
```

3.3.4. Case conversion

The **upper** and **lower** methods allow you to convert a string to uppercase or lowercase, respectively.

For example:

```
# Convert a string to uppercase using the "upper" method
s6 = s5.upper()
print(s6)  # Output: "HELLO, PYTHON!"

# Convert a string to lowercase using the "lower" method
s7 = s6.lower()
print(s7)  # Output: "hello, python!"
```

3.3.5.   Whitespace removal

The **strip** method allows you to remove leading and trailing whitespace from a string.

For example:

```
# Remove leading and trailing whitespace from a string using the "strip"
method
s8 = "    Hello, World!    "
s9 = s8.strip()
print(s9)  # Output: "Hello, World!"
```

3.3.6.   Splitting

The **split** method allows you to split a string into a list of sub-strings based on a specified delimiter.

For example:

```
# Split a string into a list of sub-strings based on a delimiter
s10 = "Hello, World!"
s11 = s10.split(", ")
print(s11)  # Output: ["Hello", "World!"]
```

3.3.7.   Searching

The **find** method allows you to search for a sub-string within a string and return the index of the first occurrence of the sub-string.

For example:

```
# Search for a sub-string within a string and return its index using the
"find" method
s12 = s10.find("World")
```

```
print(s12)  # Output: 7
```

3.3.8. Formatting

Formatting refers to the operation of inserting values into a string template. In Python, you can use the **format** method or the f-string syntax to insert values into a string template.

The **format** method allows you to specify placeholders in the string template using curly braces (**{}**). You can then pass the values to be inserted as arguments to the format method.

The f-string syntax allows you to directly insert values into the string template using the **"f"** prefix and curly braces (**{}**). You can insert variables, expressions, or even call functions within the curly braces.

```
# Insert values into a string template using the "format" method
s13 = "Hello, {}!"
s14 = s13.format("Python")
print(s14)  # Output: "Hello, Python!"

# Insert values into a string template using the f-string syntax
name = "Python"
s15 = f"Hello, {name}!"
print(s15)  # Output: "Hello, Python!"
```

3.4. Booleans

3.4.1. Overview

In Python, a boolean is a data type that can have one of two values: True or False. These values are often used in conditional statements, which allow a program to take different actions based on whether a certain condition is met.

3.4.2. Comparison operation

Booleans are often used in comparison operations, which compare two values and return a boolean value based on the result of the comparison. For example:

```
x = 5
y = 10
```

```
result = x < y  # result is True
```

In the example above, the comparison **x < y** checks if the value of x is less than the value of y. Since 5 is indeed less than 10, the comparison returns **True**. If the comparison had returned **False**, it would mean that the value of x was not less than the value of y.

Booleans can also be used in logical operations, such as **and**, **or**, and **not**. These operations allow you to test multiple conditions at the same time and return a boolean value based on the result of the tests.

For example:

```
x = 5
y = 10
z = 15

result = x < y and y < z  # result is True
```

In the example above, the **and** operator checks if both conditions **x < y** and **y < z** are true. Since both conditions are indeed true, the comparison returns **True**. If either condition had been False, the overall comparison would have returned **False**.

3.5. Numbers

3.5.1. Overview

In Python, there are three main types of numbers:

- **Integers**: These are whole numbers, such as "1", "-5", or "100". They can be positive or negative, and can be of any size (subject to the limits of your computer's memory).
- **Floating-point numbers**: These are numbers with a decimal point, such as "3.14", "-0.5", or "1.1e5". They can also be positive or negative, and can have a very large or small range (again, subject to the limits of your computer's memory).
- **Complex numbers**: These are numbers with both a real and an imaginary part, represented as **a + bj**, where a is the real part and b is the imaginary part.
  For example, "6 + 3j" is a complex number with a real part of 6 and an imaginary part of 3.

3.5.2.   int, float, complex

Numbers are a fundamental data type in Python, used to represent numeric values such as integers, floating-point numbers, and complex numbers. There are several built-in functions and methods available for working with numbers in Python.

To create an **integer (int)**, as we have seen, you can simply assign a whole number to a variable:

```
x = 10
```

To create a **floating-point** number (**float**), you can use a decimal point:

```
x = 1.37
```

To create a **complex** number, you can use the complex() function:

```
x = complex(1, 2)  # 1 + 2j
```

You can perform basic arithmetic operations on numbers using the standard arithmetic operators:

```
x = 5
y = 3
print(x + y)    # 8
print(x - y)    # 2
print(x * y)    # 15
print(x / y)    # 1.6666666666666667
print(x // y)   # 1
print(x % y)    # 2
print(x ** y)   # 125
```

3.5.3.   Built-in functions

Python also provides a number of built-in functions for working with numbers. For example, you can use the **abs()** function to find the absolute value of a number, the **round()** function to round a number to a given precision, and the **max()** and **min()** functions to find the maximum and minimum of a set of numbers, respectively.

For example:

```
x = -5
y = 3.14
z = 1.5

result = abs(x)  # result is 5
result = round(y)  # result is 3
result = max(x, y, z)  # result is 3.14
result = min(x, y, z)  # result is -5
```

3.5.4. Mathematics

You can also use the math module to perform more advanced mathematical operations such as trigonometry, logarithms, and square roots:

```
import math

x = math.pi
print(math.sin(x))  # 0.0015926529164868282
print(math.cos(x))  # -0.9999987317275395
print(math.tan(x))  # -0.0015926535896604847
print(math.sqrt(x)) # 1.7724538509055159
```

Numbers are an essential part of Python programming and are widely used to represent and manipulate numeric data in a variety of applications.

3.6. Variable conversion

Sometimes, you might need to convert a value from one type to another. Python provides built-in functions for converting values from one type to another.

For example, you can use the **int** function to convert a **float** or a **string** to an integer:

```
x = 10.5
y = int(x)  # y is now 10

x = '123'
y = int(x)  # y is now 123
```

You can use the **float** function to convert an integer or a string to a float:

```
x = 10
y = float(x)  # y is now 10.0
```

```
x = '3.14'
y = float(x)  # y is now 3.14
```

You can use the **str** function to convert any value to a string:

```
x = 10
y = str(x)  # y is now '10'

x = 3.14
y = str(x)  # y is now '3.14'

x = True
y = str(x)  # y is now 'True'
```

It is important to note that some type conversions are not possible. For example, you cannot convert a string to a boolean or vice versa.

3.7.   Users inputs

In Python, you can use the **input()** function to allow users to input data into a program. The **input()** function reads a line of text from the user and stores it in a variable as a **string**.

```
age = input("Please enter your age: ")
age = int(age)  # Convert the string to an integer
print("Your age is:", age)
```

This code prompts the user to enter their age and stores it as a string. The string is then converted to an integer using the **int()** function, and the age is printed to the console.

It's important to note that the **input()** function will always return a string, even if the user enters numerical data. This means that you will need to use type conversion if you want to work with numerical data in your program.

3.8.   Pro-Trip: Good practices for Variables

It is a good practice to choose descriptive and meaningful names for your variables. This makes your code easier to read and understand.

In Python, variable names are case-sensitive, which means that x and X are different variables. It is also a good practice to follow the **PEP 8 style guide**[1] for Python, which recommends using lowercase letters and separating words in variable names with underscores.

For example, the following are good variable names:

```
name
student_id
total_price
```

The following are not good variable names because they do not follow the recommended style or because they are reserved words:

Examples	Problems
NAME	Uppercase letters are not recommended
studentID	Underscores are not used to separate words
total-price	Dashes are not allowed in variable names
print	Print is a reserved word

[1] PEP 8 style guide for Python
https://www.python.org/dev/peps/pep-0008/

Chapter 4: Operators

4.1. Arithmetic operators

Arithmetic operators are a type of operator in Python that perform mathematical operations on numeric values. These operators include addition (+), subtraction (-), multiplication (*), division (/), floor division (//), modulus (%), and exponentiation (**). They can be used to perform basic math operations such as adding two numbers together, finding the difference between two numbers, or raising a number to a power. Arithmetic operators are essential tools for performing mathematical calculations in Python and are widely used in a variety of applications.

Below are the most common with practical examples:

```python
# Addition
x = 3 + 4  # x is 7

# Subtraction
y = 10 - 6  # y is 4

# Multiplication
z = 2 * 5  # z is 10

# Division
a = 8 / 4  # a is 2.0

# Floor division (divides and rounds down to the nearest whole number)
b = 8 // 4  # b is 2

# Modulus (returns the remainder of the division)
c = 8 % 4  # c is 0

# Exponentiation (raises a number to a power)
d = 2 ** 3  # d is 8
```

4.2. Assignment operators

Assignment operators are a type of operator in Python that are used to assign a value to a variable. These operators include the basic **assignment operator (=)**, as well as shorthand operators for performing arithmetic operations and assigning the result to a variable in a single step. For example, the **+= operator** can be used to add a value to a variable and assign the result to that variable in a single statement. Similarly, the **-=, *=, /=, //=, %=,** and ****= operators** can be used to subtract, multiply, divide, floor divide, modulus, and exponentiate, respectively, and assign the result to a variable. Assignment operators are often used to update the value of a variable based on some calculation or to simplify complex assignment statements.

Assignment operators are an important part of Python programming, as they allow you to assign a value to a variable. They are used to store values in memory so that you can use them later in your program. There are several types of assignment operators available in Python, each of which performs a specific task.

The basic assignment operator (=) is used to assign a value to a variable. For example, you can use it to assign an integer value to a variable like this:

```
x = 5
```

In this example, the value 5 is being assigned to the variable x. You can also use the assignment operator to assign the result of an expression to a variable. For example:

```
x = 2 + 3
```

In this case, the value of the expression 2 + 3 is being assigned to the variable x.

In addition to the basic assignment operator, Python also provides a number of shorthand assignment operators that allow you to perform an arithmetic operation and assign the result to a variable in a single statement.

For example, the += operator can be used to add a value to a variable and assign the result to that variable in a single statement.

Here's an example:

```
x = 5
x += 3   # x is now 8
```

Similarly, the -= operator can be used to subtract a value from a variable, the *= operator can be used to multiply a variable by a value, and so on.

Below are more practical examples:

```
# Multiply and assign
x *= 4   # x is now 24

# Divide and assign
x /= 6   # x is now 4.0
```

```
# Floor divide and assign
x //= 2   # x is now 2

# Modulus and assign
x %= 3   # x is now 2

# Exponent and assign
x **= 3   # x is now 8
```

Assignment operators are a useful and efficient way to update the value of a variable based on some calculation or to simplify complex assignment statements. They are widely used in Python programs to store and manipulate data.

4.3. Comparison operators

Comparison operators are a type of operator in Python that are used to compare two values and determine whether a specific relationship exists between them. These operators include equal to (==), not equal to (!=), greater than (>), less than (<), greater than or equal to (>=), and less than or equal to (<=). They return a Boolean value of True or False based on the comparison.

For example, the equal to operator (==) can be used to determine if two values are equal:

```
x = 5
y = 5
print(x == y)   # True
```

In this example, the values of x and y are both 5, so the comparison evaluates to True.

On the other hand, the not equal to operator (!=) can be used to determine if two values are not equal:

```
x = 5
y = 6
print(x != y)   # True
```

In this example, the values of x and y are different, so the comparison evaluates to True.

Comparison operators are often used in conditional statements to control the flow of a program based on the outcome of a comparison. For example, you might use a comparison operator in an if statement to check if a value is greater than or equal to another value:

```
x = 5
if x >= 3:
    print("x is greater than or equal to 3")
```

In this case, the comparison x >= 3 evaluates to True, so the message "x is greater than or equal to 3" is printed to the screen.

Below are additional practical examples:

```
# Test values
x = 4
y = 5

print(x == y)  # False

# Not equal to
print(x != y)  # True

# Greater than
print(x > y)  # False

# Less than
print(x < y)  # True

# Greater than or equal to
print(x >= y)  # False

# Less than or equal to
print(x <= y)  # True
```

These operators compare two values and return a **Boolean** value (**True** or **False**) based on the comparison.

Comparison operators are a powerful tool for comparing values and making decisions in your Python programs. They are widely used in a variety of applications to compare and manipulate data.

4.4. Logical operators

Logical operators are a type of operator in Python that are used to perform logical operations on Boolean values. These operators include logical **AND** (and), logical **OR** (or), and logical **NOT** (not). They are used to combine or negate Boolean values in order to make more complex decisions in your program.

The logical **AND** operator (and) is used to determine if both of two Boolean values are **True**:

```
x = True
y = True
print(x and y)   # True
```

In this example, both x and y are **True**, so the expression x and y evaluates to **True**.

On the other hand, the logical **OR** operator (or) is used to determine if at least one of two Boolean values is **True**:

```
x = True
y = False
print(x or y)   # True
```

In this example, x is **True**, so the expression x or y evaluates to True.

The logical **NOT** operator (not) is used to negate a Boolean value:

```
x = True
print(not x)   # False
```

In this example, the value of x is **True**, so the expression not x evaluates to False.

Logical operators are often used in conjunction with comparison operators to make more complex decisions in your program.

For example, you might use a combination of logical and comparison operators in an if statement to check multiple conditions:

```
x = 5
y = 10
if x > 3 and y < 20:
    print("x is greater than 3 and y is less than 20")
```

In this case, the expression x > 3 and y < 20 evaluates to True, so the message "x is greater than 3 and y is less than 20" is printed to the screen.

Logical operators are an important part of Python programming and are widely used to combine and negate Boolean values in order to make more complex decisions in your programs.

4.5. Identity operators

Identity operators are a type of operator in Python that are used to compare the memory location of two objects. These operators include **is** and **is not**. They return a Boolean value of **True** or **False** based on whether the two objects being compared are the same or not.

The is operator is used to determine if two variables refer to the same object:

```
x = [1, 2, 3]
y = x
print(x is y)   # True
```

In this example, the variables x and y both refer to the same object, a list containing the values 1, 2, and 3. Therefore, the expression x is y evaluates to **True**.

On the other hand, the is not operator is used to determine if two variables do not refer to the same object:

```
x = [1, 2, 3]
y = [1, 2, 3]
print(x is not y)   # True
```

In this example, the variables x and y both contain the same values, but they refer to different objects in memory. Therefore, the expression x is not y evaluates to **True**.

Identity operators are useful for determining if two variables refer to the same object, which can be important in certain situations. For example, you might use the is operator to check if a variable is pointing to **None**, like this:

```
x = None
if x is None:
    print("x is None")
```

In this case, the expression x is **None** evaluates to **True**, so the message "x is None" is printed to the screen.

Identity operators are an important part of Python programming and are often used to compare the memory location of objects in order to make decisions in your program.

4.6. Membership operators

Membership operators are a type of operator in Python that are used to check if a value is contained in a sequence (such as a list or a string). These operators include **in** and **not in**. They return a **Boolean** value of **True** or **False** based on whether the value being checked is contained in the sequence or not.

```
# Check if a value is in a sequence
x = [1, 2, 3]
print(1 in x)   # True
```

In this example, the value 1 is contained in the list x, so the expression 1 in x evaluates to **True**.

On the other hand, the not in operator is used to check if a value is not contained in a sequence:

```
# Check if a value is not in a sequence
x = "Talence"
print("T" not in x)   # False
```

In this example, the value "h" is contained in the string x, so the expression "h" not in x evaluates to **False**.

Membership operators are often used to check if a value is contained in a sequence before performing some action. For example, you might use the **in** operator in a **for** loop to iterate over the elements of a list:

```
x = [1, 2, 3]
for value in x:
    print(value)
```

In this case, the **in** operator is used to check if each element of the list x is contained in the sequence, and the **for** loop prints each element to the screen.

Membership operators are a useful tool for checking if a value is contained in a sequence and are widely used in Python programs to manipulate and iterate over data.

You can also use a step value to skip elements in the slice. The syntax is **lst[start:end:step]**.

For example:

```
# Extract every other element from the list [1, 2, 3, 4, 5]
sub_list = lst[::2]
print(sub_list)  # Output: [1, 3, 5]
```

5.1.3.   Change or add values

Lists are mutable in Python, which means that you can change the elements of a list once it has been created. Here are some examples of how to modify a list:

For example:

```
# Create a list of integers
my_list = [1, 2, 3]

# Change the value of the first item
my_list[0] = 10
print(my_list)  # Output: [10, 2, 3]

# Add a new item to the end of the list
my_list.append(4)
print(my_list)  # Output: [10, 2, 3, 4]

# Insert a new item at a specific index
my_list.insert(1, 5)
print(my_list)  # Output: [10, 5, 2, 3, 4]

# Add multiple items to the end of the list using the extend method
my_list.extend([6, 7, 8])
print(my_list)  # Output: [10, 5, 2, 3, 4, 6, 7, 8]

# Replace a range of items using slicing
my_list[2:4] = [20, 30]
print(my_list)  # Output: [10, 5, 20, 30, 4, 6, 7, 8]
```

5.1.4.   Pro Tips: When to use Lists

In Python, a list is an ordered collection of items that can be of any data type (including other lists). Lists are useful when you need to store and retrieve a collection of items in a specific order.

You might want to use a list in Python when you need to store a collection of items that needs to be in a specific order, and you want to be able to easily add, remove, or modify the items in the list.

In general, lists are a useful data structure in Python whenever you need to store and retrieve a collection of items in a specific order, and you want to be able to easily add, remove, or modify the items in the list. They are particularly useful when working with data that needs to be processed in a specific order, such as in a loop.

Note that Python also has another data structure called a tuple, which is similar to a list but is immutable (i.e., you cannot modify the elements of a tuple once it is created). Tuples are often used when you need to store a collection of items that should not be modified, such as the elements of a point (x, y) in a 2D coordinate system.

5.2. Tuples

5.2.1. What are Tuples?

In Python, a **tuple** is an immutable sequence type. This means that once you create a tuple, you cannot change its contents. Tuples are created using parentheses ( ) or by using the tuple function.

Tuples are similar to lists, but they are immutable, which means that once you create a tuple, you cannot change its elements. This makes tuples more efficient for storing data that does not need to be modified, but it also means that you cannot use many of the methods that are available for lists.

To create a tuple in Python, you can use parentheses and separate the elements with commas.

For example:

```
my_tuple = (1, 2, 3)
```

Tuples also have a number of built-in methods, but they are more limited than the methods available for lists. Some common methods include **count()**, which counts the number of occurrences of a given element, and **index()**, which returns the index of the first occurrence of a given element.

5.2.2. Access elements

We can access the items in a tuple using their index, just like we do with lists. The index of the first item in a tuple is 0, and the index of the second item is 1, and so on.

We can access an item in a tuple by using its index in square brackets, like this:

```
first_item = my_tuple[0]
second_item = my_tuple[1]
```

You can also use negative indices to access items from the end of the tuple. For example, the index -1 refers to the last item in the tuple, -2 refers to the second to last item, and so on.

```
last_item = my_tuple[-1]
second_to_last_item = my_tuple[-2]
```

5.2.3. Mixing types

Tuples can contain items of different types, just like lists. However, unlike lists, tuples are immutable, which means that you cannot change the values of individual items or add or remove items from a tuple.

Here is an example of a tuple containing integers, strings, and a float:

```
my_tuple = (1, 'hello', 3.14)
```

We can also create a tuple by enclosing a comma-separated sequence of values in parentheses:

```
my_tuple = 1, 'hello', 3.14
```

5.2.4. Tuple Slicing

Just like with lists, you can access a range of items in a tuple using slicing. Slicing is done using the colon (:) operator. For example, to get the first two items in a tuple, you can use the following slice:

```
first_two_items = my_tuple[0:2]
```

This will return a new tuple containing the items at indices 0 and 1. You can also omit the first index to start from the beginning of the tuple, or the second index to slice to the end of the tuple.

For example, the following will return a new tuple containing all the items in my_tuple except for the last one:

```
all_but_last = my_tuple[:-1]
```

5.2.5. Tuple Unpacking

You can "unpack" a tuple into separate variables by assigning the tuple to a comma-separated list of variables.

For example:

```
x, y, z = my_tuple
```

will assign the values of the items in my_tuple to the variables x, y, and z, respectively.

5.2.6. Tuple Methods and Functions

There are a few methods and functions that you can use with tuples.

The **len** function returns the length of the tuple:

```
tuple_length = len(my_tuple)
```

The **count** method returns the number of times a specific value appears in the tuple:

```
hello_count = my_tuple.count('hello')
```

The **index** method returns the index of the first occurrence of a specific value in the tuple:

```
hello_index = my_tuple.index('hello')
```

You can also use the **in** operator to check if a specific value is contained in the tuple:

```
if 'hello' in my_tuple:
    print('Hello is in the tuple')
```

5.2.7. Pro Tips: When to use Tuples

Tuples are useful when you need to store a fixed set of values that you don't want to change.

For example, you might use a tuple to store a person's name and age:

```
person = ('Alice', 25)
```

Because tuples are **immutable**, you can use them as keys in dictionaries and as elements in sets. Lists, on the other hand, are not suitable for these purposes because they are mutable.

Tuples are also more memory-efficient than lists because they do not require the extra overhead for changing their size.

5.3. Dictionaries

5.3.1. What are Dictionaries?

Dictionaries are a fundamental data type in Python, and are used to store **key-value pairs**. They are similar to lists, but instead of using integers to index values, dictionaries use keys, which can be any **immutable** type (such as strings or numbers).

Dictionaries are also known as associative arrays or hash maps.

Dictionaries are created using curly braces (**{}**), and the key-value pairs are separated by a colon (:). Keys must be unique, and they can be of any immutable type (such as strings, integers, or tuples with immutable elements). Values can be of any type.

Here is an example of a dictionary containing three key-value pairs:

```
my_dict = {'name': 'Alice', 'age': 25, 'city': 'New York'}
```

You can also create a dictionary using the dict function:

```
my_dict = dict(name='Alice', age=25, city='New York')
```

5.3.2. Accessing Dictionary Items

To access the values in a dictionary, you can use the square brackets [] and the **key**.

For example, to access the **value** for the 'name' **key**:

```
my_dict = dict(name='Alice', age=25, city='New York')
name = my_dict['name']   # name is 'Alice'
age = my_dict['age']     # age is 25
```

If you try to access a key that does not exist in the dictionary, you will get a **KeyError exception**. You can use the get method to avoid this exception.

The **get** method returns the value for a key if it exists, or a **default value** if it does not:

You can also use the **get()** method to access values.

This is useful because it returns a default value (such as **None**) if the key does not exist in the dictionary:

```
my_dict = dict(name='Alice', age=25, city='New York')
city = my_dict.get('city')
print(city) # Print 'New York'

country = my_dict.get('country', 'United States')
print(country) # Print 'United States' (default value)
```

Note: This will output 'United States', because the 'country' key does not exist in the dictionary and the default value of 'United States' is returned instead.

5.3.3. Add / Delete / Update key-value pairs

To add or update key-value pairs in a dictionary, you can use the assignment operator **=**. For example, to add a new key-value pair for the 'country' key:

```
my_dict['country'] = 'United States'
print(my_dict)
```

This will add a new key-value pair to the dictionary, with the key being 'country' and the value being 'United States'.

To delete a key-value pair from a dictionary, you can use the del statement. For example, to delete the 'age' key-value pair:

```
del my_dict['age']
print(my_dict)
```

This will remove the 'age' key and its associated value from the dictionary.

You can also use the **pop()** method to remove a key-value pair and return its value. This is useful if you want to save the value before deleting it. For example:

```
age = my_dict.pop('age', None)
print(age)
```

This will output None, because the 'age' key does not exist in the dictionary. However, if we had a key-value pair for 'age', it would be removed from the dictionary and its value would be returned.

5.3.4.   List all keys

To list all the keys in a Python dictionary, you can use the **keys()** method. This method returns a view object that contains the keys of the dictionary, which you can then iterate over using a for loop or convert to a list using the **list()** function.

Here is an example of how to use the **keys()** method to list all the keys in a dictionary:

```
my_dict = {'a': 1, 'b': 2, 'c': 3}

# Use the keys() method to get a view object of the dictionary's keys
keys = my_dict.keys()

# Iterate over the keys and print them
for key in keys:
    print(key)
```

This will output:

```
a
b
c
```

We can also convert the keys to a list and print the list (same dictionary):

```
key_list = list(keys)
print(key_list)
```

This will output:

```
['a', 'b', 'c']
```

5.3.5. Dictionaries built-in methods

Dictionaries also have a number of built-in methods:

Dictionaries also have a number of built-in methods that you can use to modify and query them. Some of the most commonly used methods are:

- **dict.clear()**: Removes all items from the dictionary.
- **dict.copy()**: Returns a shallow copy of the dictionary.
- **dict.get(key[, default])**: Returns the value for the given key, or the default value if the key is not found.
- **dict.items()**: Returns a view object that displays a list of the dictionary's key-value pairs.
- **dict.keys()**: Returns a view object that displays a list of the dictionary's keys.
- **dict.pop(key[, default])**: Removes the specified key and returns its value, or the default value if the key is not found.
- **dict.popitem()**: Removes and returns an arbitrary key-value pair from the dictionary.
- **dict.setdefault(key[, default])**: Returns the value for the given key, or the default value if the key is not found, and also sets the default value for the key if it is not found.
- **dict.update(other_dict)**: Updates the dictionary with the key-value pairs from the other dictionary. If a key is present in both dictionaries, the value from the other dictionary is used.
- **dict.values()**: Returns a view object that displays a list of the dictionary's values.

```
# Create a dictionary
d = {'a': 1, 'b': 2, 'c': 3}

# Get the value for the key 'b'
value = d.get('b')  # returns 2

# Set the value for the key 'd' to 4
```

```
d['d'] = 4

# Update the dictionary with the key-value pairs from another dictionary
other_dict = {'e': 5, 'f': 6}
d.update(other_dict)

# Remove the key-value pair for the key 'a'
d.pop('a')

# Remove an arbitrary key-value pair
key, value = d.popitem()

# Clear the dictionary
d.clear()
```

5.3.6. Pro-Tips: When to use Dictionaries

You might want to use a dictionary in Python when you have a set of data that needs to be stored and retrieved efficiently, and you want to access the data using keys rather than indices.

For example, you might use a dictionary to store a set of user records, where the keys are the user IDs and the values are the user information (such as name, age, and location).

Here is an more advanced example of how to create and use a dictionary in Python:

```
# Create a dictionary
user_data = {
    "user1": {"name": "Alice", "age": 25, "city": "New York"},
    "user2": {"name": "Bob", "age": 27, "city": "Paris"},
    "user3": {"name": "Charlie", "age": 30, "city": "San Francisco"}
}

# Access a value using its key
user1_name = user_data["user1"]["name"]
print(f"Name: {user1_name}")

# Update a value using its key
user_data["user2"]["age"] = 26

# Add a new key-value pair
user_data["user4"] = {"name": "Frank", "age": 35, "city": "Chicago"}

# Iterate over the keys and values in the dictionary
for user_id, user_info in user_data.items():
    print(f"{user_id}: {user_info}")
```

Below is the result:

```
Name: Alice
user1: {'name': 'Alice', 'age': 25, 'city': 'New York'}
user2: {'name': 'Bob', 'age': 26, 'city': 'Paris'}
user3: {'name': 'Charlie', 'age': 30, 'city': 'San Francisco'}
user4: {'name': 'Frank', 'age': 35, 'city': 'Chicago'}
```

Chapter 6: Control structures

6.1.   if / elif / else statements

If statements are a fundamental aspect of programming that allow you to execute different blocks of code based on whether a condition is true or false. In Python, an if statement is written as follows:

```python
if condition:
    # code to execute if condition is True
```

The condition is a boolean expression that evaluates to either True or False. If the condition is True, the code block indented under the if statement is executed. If the condition is False, the code block is skipped.

Here is an example of an if statement in action:

```python
x = 5
if x > 0:
    print("x is positive")
```

This code will print "x is positive" to the console because the condition **x > 0** is True.

You can also add an optional else clause to an if statement, which will execute a code block if the condition is False:

```python
x = 5
if x > 0:
    print("x is positive")
else:
    print("x is not positive")
```

This code will also print "x is positive" to the console because the condition **x > 0** is True.

You can also include additional conditions using the **elif** keyword, which stands for "else if". This allows you to check multiple conditions and execute different code blocks depending on which condition is True:

```python
x = 5
if x > 0:
```

```
    print("x is positive")
elif x < 0:
    print("x is negative")
else:
    print("x is zero")
```

In this example, the code will print "x is positive" to the console because the first condition, **x > 0**, is True.

It's important to note that once a condition is True, the rest of the conditions and code blocks are skipped. For example, in the above code, even if the second condition **x < 0** were True, the code block under the elif clause would not be executed because the first condition is already True.

You can also nest if statements within each other to create more complex conditional logic. For example:

```
x = 5
y = 10

if x > 0:
    if y > 0:
        print("both x and y are positive")
    else:
        print("x is positive but y is not")
else:
    print("x is not positive")
```

In this example, the code will print "both x and y are positive" to the console because both conditions are True.

If statements are an essential tool for controlling the flow of your program and making decisions based on data. By using if statements, you can write programs that can adapt and behave differently based on the input and conditions you define.

6.2. for loops

6.2.1. What are for loops?

For loops are a fundamental aspect of programming that allow you to repeat a block of code a specific number of times. In Python, a **for** loop is written as follows:

```
for variable in sequence:
```

```
# code to be executed
```

The **for** keyword indicates the start of the loop, variable is a variable that takes on the value of each element in the sequence, and sequence is a list of elements that the loop will iterate over.

6.2.2.   Iterating over a range of numbers

One common use case for **for** loops is to iterate over a range of numbers. You can use the **range()** function to generate a sequence of numbers to iterate over. The **range()** function takes three arguments: **start**, **stop**, and **step**:

- **start** is the starting value of the **range** (inclusive)
- **stop** is the ending value of the range (exclusive)
- **step** is the interval between each number in the range

Here are some examples of using the **range()** function:

```
# Iterate over a range of numbers from 0 to 9
for i in range(10):
    print(i)

# Iterate over a range of numbers from 1 to 10
for i in range(1, 11):
    print(i)

# Iterate over a range of numbers from 0 to 9 with a step of 2
for i in range(0, 10, 2):
    print(i)
```

6.2.3.   Iterating over a list

You can use a for loop to iterate over a list of elements by using the syntax "**for element in list:**".

For example:

```
fruits = ['apple', 'grape', 'watermelon']
for fruit in fruits:
    print(fruit)
```

6.2.4. Iterating over a string

You can also use a for loop to iterate over the characters in a string by using the syntax "**for character in string:**".

For example:

```
string = "hello"
for c in string:
    print(c)
```

This code will print each character in the string to the console.

6.2.5. Using the enumerate function

Sometimes you may want to loop over a list and access both the index and the value of each element. You can use the **enumerate()** function to do this. The **enumerate()** function returns a tuple for each iteration, where the first element is the index and the second element is the value.

Here is an example of using the **enumerate()** function:

```
fruits = ['apple', 'grape', 'watermelon']
for i, fruit in enumerate(fruits):
    print(i, fruit)
```

This code will print the index and value of each element in the list to the console.

6.2.6. Using the zip function

The **zip()** function allows you to iterate over multiple lists at the same time. The **zip()** function returns a tuple for each iteration, where the elements of the tuple come from the corresponding elements of the input lists.

Here is an example of using the **zip()** function:

```
names = ['Alice', 'Bob', 'Charlie']
ages = [25, 27, 30]

for name, age in zip(names, ages):
    print(name, age)
```

This code will print the name and age for each person in the lists to the console.

6.2.7. The for-else loop

The **for-else** loop is a combination of a **for** loop and an **else** clause. The **else** clause is executed after the loop has completed, but only if the loop completed normally (i.e., not as the result of a break statement).

Here is an example of a for-else loop:

```python
numbers = [1, 2, 3, 4, 5]
for number in numbers:
    if number % 2 == 0:
        print(number, "is even")
        break
else:
    print("No even numbers in this iteration")
```

In this example, the loop will print "2 is even" and then exit because the **break** statement is encountered when number is 2. The else clause will not be executed because the loop was not completed normally.

If you remove the **break** statement, the loop will complete normally and the **else** clause will be executed, printing "*No even numbers in this iteration*" to the console.

6.2.8. Conclusion

For loops are a powerful and flexible tool for iterating over sequences and performing actions in your program. By using for loops and the various functions and techniques described above, you can write programs that can automate tasks and process data efficiently.

6.3. while loops

6.3.1. What are while loops?

Python also has a **while** loop - in addition to the **for** keyword - which allows you to execute a code block while a condition is True. The syntax for a while loop is as follows:

```python
while condition:
```

```
# code to be executed
```

The **while** keyword indicates the start of the loop, and condition is a boolean expression that determines whether the loop should continue. If the condition is True, the code block indented under the while loop is executed, and the condition is checked again.

This process continues until the condition becomes False, at which point the loop is exited.

Here is an example of a **while** loop in action:

```
x = 10
while x > 0:
    print(x)
    x = x - 1
```

This code will print the numbers 10 through 1 to the console because the condition **x > 0** is True for each iteration, and the value of **x** is decreased by 1 each time the loop is executed.

You can also use the **break** keyword to exit a loop prematurely and the **continue** keyword to skip the rest of the current iteration and move on to the next one. We will detail this.

6.3.2. Using the break keyword

You can use the **break** keyword to exit a while loop prematurely. When the break keyword is encountered, the loop is immediately exited and the program continues with the next line of code following the loop.

Here is an example of using the **break** keyword:

```
x = 0
while True:
    x = x + 1
    if x > 5:
        break
    print(x)
```

This code will print the numbers 1 through 5 to the console and then exit the loop because the **break** keyword is encountered when x becomes greater than 5.

6.3.3.   Using the continue keyword

You can use the **continue** keyword to skip the rest of the current iteration and move on to the next one. When the continue keyword is encountered, the program immediately jumps back to the top of the loop and reevaluates the condition.

Here is an example of using the **continue** keyword:

```
x = 0
while x < 10:
    x = x + 1
    if x % 2 == 0:
        continue
    print(x)
```

This code will print the odd numbers from 1 to 9 to the console because the **continue** keyword is encountered for even numbers, causing the program to skip the rest of the current iteration and move on to the next one.

6.3.4.   The while-else loop

The **while-else** loop is similar to the **for-else** loop, but with a **while** loop instead of a **for** loop. The **else** clause is executed after the loop has completed, but only if the loop completed normally (i.e., not as the result of a break statement).

Here is an example of a **while-else** loop:

```
x = 0
while x < 5:
    x = x + 1
    if x % 2 == 0:
        print(x, "is even")
        break
else:
    print("No even numbers in this iteration")
```

In this example, the loop will print "2 is even" and then exit because the **break** statement is encountered when **x** is 2. The else clause will not be executed because the loop was not completed normally.

If you remove the **break** statement, the loop will complete normally and the else clause will be executed, printing "*No even numbers in this iteration*" to the console.

6.3.5. The infinite loop

An infinite loop is a loop that never stops executing. You can create an infinite loop by using the **while True** syntax.

Here is an example of an infinite loop:

```python
while True:
    print("Hello World!")
```

This code will print "*Hello World!*" to the console **indefinitely** because the condition **True** is always true.

Infinite loops are generally not recommended because they can cause your program to run forever and consume resources indefinitely. However, they can be useful in certain situations, such as in server programs that need to run continuously and wait for input.

6.3.6. Conclusion

In summary, Python provides several looping constructs to allow you to repeat actions and control the flow of your program. You can choose the appropriate looping construct based on your specific needs and the requirements of your program.

Chapter 7: Functions

7.1. Defining and calling functions

7.1.1. What is a function?

Functions are a fundamental aspect of programming that allow you to **group** and **reuse** code. In Python, a function is a block of code that performs a specific task and can be called by other parts of your program.

7.1.2. Defining a function

To define a function in Python, you use the **def** keyword followed by the function name and a set of parentheses that may contain parameters. The code block indented under the function definition is the body of the function.

Here is an example of a function definition in Python:

```python
def hello():
    print("Hello World!")
```

This function definition creates a function called **hello** that prints *"Hello World!"* to the console. The function will not be used at this time, but we will utilize it in the next section.

7.1.3. Calling a function

To call a function in Python, you use the function name followed by a set of parentheses that may contain arguments.

For example:

```python
def hello():
    print("Hello World!")

hello() # Print "Hello World!"
```

This will call the function called **hello** that prints *"Hello World!"* to the console.

7.2. Parameters and arguments

7.2.1. Overview

Parameters are variables that are defined in the function definition and act as placeholders for the values that are passed to the function when it is called. Arguments are the actual values that are passed to the function when it is called. You can define multiple parameters in a function by separating them with a comma.

For example, we can improve our **hello()** function which will be able to handle a first name and a last name:

```
def hello(firstname, lastname):
    print("Hello, my first name is", firstname, "and my last name is",
lastname, ".")

hello("John", "Doe") # Print "Hello, my first name is John and my last
name is Doe."
```

This function definition creates a function called **hello** that takes two parameters: **firstname** (John) and **lastname** (Doe). When the function is called, the arguments passed to the function are used to fill in the values of the parameters.

7.2.2. Default parameter values

You can specify default values for parameters in the function definition. If an argument is not passed to the function when it is called, the default value will be used instead.

For example:

```
def hello(name="Alice"):
    print("Hi", name)

hello()       # Print "Hi Alice"
hello("Bob") # Print "Hi Bob"
```

This code defines a function called **hello** that takes a single parameter name with a default value of "Alice". When the function is called without any arguments, the default value of "Alice" is used.

When the function is called with the argument "Bob", the value of "Bob" is used.

This code will print "*Hi Alice*" and "*Hi Bob*" to the console.

7.2.3. Variable length arguments

Sometimes, you may not know in advance how many arguments a function will need to accept. In this case, you can use variable length arguments to allow the function to accept any number of arguments.

In Python, you can use the *** operator** to define a function with variable length arguments. The *** operator** allows you to specify that the function should accept any number of arguments, and it stores them in a tuple called **args**.

For example:

```python
def hello(*names):
    for name in names:
        print("Hi", name)

greet("Alice", "Bob", "Charlie")
```

This code defines a function called **hello** that takes a variable length argument called **names**. When the function is called, it iterates over the tuple of names and prints a greeting to the console for each name.

You can also use the **** operator** to define a function with variable length keyword arguments. The **** operator** allows you to specify that the function should accept any number of keyword arguments, and it stores them in a dictionary called **kwargs**.

For example:

```python
def hello(**kwargs):
    for name, age in kwargs.items():
        print("Hello", name, "are you", age, "years old?")

hello(Alice=25, Bob=27, Charlie=30)
```

This code defines a function called **hello** that takes a variable length argument called **kwargs**. When the function is called, it iterates over the dictionary of keyword arguments and prints a greeting to the console for each one.

7.3. Return values

A function can return a value to the caller using the **return** keyword. When a function reaches a **return** statement, it immediately exits the function and returns the specified value to the caller.

For example:

```
def add(a, b):
    result = a + b
    return result

sum = add(10, 20)
print(sum) # Print "30"
```

This code defines a function called **add** that takes two parameters **a** and **b** and returns the sum of those two values.

The function is called with the arguments 5 and 10, and the returned value is assigned to the **sum** variable. The final line of code prints the value of **sum** to the console, which will be 30.

7.4. Variable scope

In Python, variables defined inside a function are local to that function and are not accessible outside of the function. Variables defined outside of a function, in the **global scope**, are accessible from within the function.

For example:

```
var = 5

def print_var():
    print(var)

print_var()
```

This code defines a global variable **var** with the value 5, and a function called **print_var** that prints the value of **var** to the console. When the function is called, it will print 5 to the console because **var** is defined in the global scope and is accessible from within the function.

If you define a variable with the same name as a global variable inside a function, the local variable will shadow the global variable, meaning that the global variable will not be accessible from within the function.

For example:

```
var = 5
```

```
def print_var():
    var = 10
    print(var)

print_var()

print(var)
```

This code defines a global variable **var** with the value 5, and a function called **print_var** that defines a local variable **var** with the value 10 and then prints the value of **var** to the console.

When the function is called, it will print 10 to the console because the local variable **var** shadows the global variable **var**. The final line of code prints the value of the global **var** to the console, which will be 5.

To access a global variable from within a function, you can use the **global** keyword to specify that you are referring to the global variable, rather than a local variable with the same name.

For example:

```
var = 5

def print_var():
    global var
    var = 10
    print(var)

print_var()
print(var)
```

This code defines a global variable **var** with the value 5, and a function called **print_var** that uses the **global** keyword to specify that it is accessing the global variable **var** and then assigns a new value of 10 to it. When the function is called, it will print 10 to the console because the global variable **var** has been modified. The final line of code prints the value of the global **var** to the console, which will also be 10.

Chapter 8: File input and output

8.1.   Overview

In Python, you can use file input and output to read from and write to files on your computer's file system. This can be useful for storing data, such as configurations or program outputs, or for reading data from external sources.

8.2.   Working with Files

8.2.1.   Reading from a File

To read from a file in Python, you can use the **open()** function, which returns a file object that you can use to access the contents of the file. The **open()** function takes two arguments: the name of the file, and the mode in which to open the file. The mode can be one of several options, such as **'r'** for reading (the default), **'w'** for writing, or **'a'** for appending.

Here's an example of how to open a file for reading:

```
with open('example.txt', 'r') as f:
    contents = f.read()
```

In this example, the **with** statement opens the file **example.txt** for reading, and assigns the resulting file object to the variable **f**.

The **read()** method of the file object reads the entire contents of the file and stores it in the **contents** variable.

The **with** statement is used here to ensure that the file is properly closed after reading, even if an exception is raised. This is known as a "context manager," and it is a good practice to use it when working with files.

Once you have read the contents of a file, you can process them as you like. For example, you might want to split the contents into lines, or search for a particular string. Here's an example of how to split the contents of a file into lines:

```
with open('example.txt', 'r') as f:
    lines = f.readlines()
```

The **readlines()** method reads the contents of the file and returns a list of strings, with each string representing a line of the file. You can then access the lines of the file using indices, like this:

```
first_line = lines[0]
second_line = lines[1]
```

8.2.2.   Writing to a File

To write to a file in Python, you can use the **open()** function with the **'w'** mode to create a new file, or the **'a'** mode to append to an existing file.

Here's an example of how to create a new file and write some data to it:

```
with open('output.txt', 'w') as f:
    f.write('This is the first line.\n')
    f.write('This is the second line.\n')
```

In this example, the **with** statement opens the file **output.txt** for writing, and assigns the resulting file object to the variable **f**. The **write()** method of the file object writes the string provided as an argument to the file.

You can also use the **writelines()** method to write a list of strings to a file, like this:

```
lines = ['This is the first line.\n', 'This is the second line.\n']

with open('output.txt', 'w') as f:
    f.writelines(lines)
```

8.2.3.   Pro-Tips: All modes for the open() function

In Python, when you use the open() function to work with files, you need to specify a mode that determines how you want to access the file.

The following are those different modes:

- 'r': This mode opens the file for reading. It is the default mode if no mode is specified.

- 'w': This mode opens the file for writing, and overwrites the file if it already exists. If the file does not exist, it is created.
- 'a': This mode opens the file for writing, and appends the new data to the end of the file if it already exists. If the file does not exist, it is created.
- 'x': This mode creates a new file for writing, and raises an error if the file already exists.
- 'b': This mode can be used in combination with any of the above modes to open the file in binary mode.
- 't': This mode can be used in combination with any of the above modes to open the file in text mode. This is the default mode if no mode is specified.

For example, to open a file for **reading** in **text mode**, you can use the following code:

```python
with open('input.txt', 'rt') as f:
    contents = f.read()
```

To open a file for **writing** in **binary mode**, you can use the following code:

```python
with open('output.bin', 'wb') as f:
    f.write(b'\x01\x02\x03')
```

8.3. Working with JSON files

8.3.1. Overview

JSON (JavaScript Object Notation) is a popular data interchange format that is used to represent structured data as a sequence of characters. It is often used for storing and exchanging data over the internet, and is natively supported by many programming languages, including Python.

In Python, you can use the **json** module to work with JSON files. This module provides functions for reading and writing JSON data, as well as for converting between JSON and other data types, such as dictionaries and lists.

8.3.2. Creating a JSON test file

To start, let's first create a JSON file. Open a text editor and create a file called "data.json" with the following contents:

```
{
    "name": "Alice",
    "age": 25,
    "city": "New York"
}
```

This is a simple JSON object with three key-value pairs: "name", "age", and "city".

8.3.3. Reading JSON Data

Now, let's open and read this JSON file in Python. First, we need to import the **json** module:

```
import json
```

Next, we can use the **open()** function to open the JSON file in reading mode, and then use the **json.load()** function to parse the contents of the file:

```
with open('data.json', 'r') as f:
    data = json.load(f)

print(data)
```

This will output the JSON object as a Python dictionary:

```
{'name': 'Alice', 'age': 25, 'city': 'New York'}
```

We can access the values in the dictionary using the keys:

```
name = data['name']
age = data['age']
city = data['city']

print(f"{name} is {age} years old and lives in {city}.")
```

This will output:

```
Alice is 25 years old and lives in New York.
```

8.3.4.   Writing JSON Data

We can also write JSON data to a file using the **json.dump()** function. First, let's create a Python dictionary with some data:

```
data = {
    "name": "Bob",
    "age": 30,
    "city": "Paris"
}
```

Next, we can open a file in writing mode and use **json.dump()** to write the data to the file:

```
with open('output.json', 'w') as f:
    json.dump(data, f)
```

This will overwrite the contents of the "**output.json**" file with the new data.

8.3.5.   Pro-Tips: Python Object / JSON String conversion

We can also use the **json.dumps()** function to convert a **Python object to a JSON string**, which can be printed or stored as a string variable:

```
json_data = json.dumps(data)
print(json_data)
```

This will output the JSON object as a string:

```
{"name": "Bob", "age": 30, "city": "Paris"}
```

We can also use the **json.loads()** function to convert a **JSON string to a Python object**:

```
data = json.loads(json_data)
print(data)
```

This will output the JSON object as a Python dictionary:

```
{'name': 'Bob', 'age': 30, 'city': 'Paris'}
```

Chapter 9: Python projects for beginners

9.1. Overview

Welcome to the hands-on projects chapter! In this chapter, you will have the opportunity to practice writing code by completing the following projects:

- Temperature converter program that allows the user to convert temperatures between Celsius and Fahrenheit.
- Simple calculator program that allows the user to perform basic arithmetic operations.
- Number guessing game program that challenges the user to guess a randomly generated number.
- Random password generator program that allows the user to specify the length and character set (e.g. digits, lowercase letters, uppercase letters, special characters) of the generated password.
- To-do list program that allows the user to create, view, and modify a list of tasks.
- Web scraper program that allows the user to specify a target website and extract specific data from it.
- Tic-tac-toe game program that allows two players to play against each other.
- Weather forecast app that allows the user to input their location and receive real-time weather data, including temperature, humidity, wind speed, and a description of the current weather conditions (using an API).

In each project, you will have the opportunity to apply the Python concepts and skills you have learned so far to solve real-world problems.

> You can find all of these projects on **GitHub** at the following URL:
> https://github.com/TalenceInstitute/Python-Beginners-Projects

Let's get started!

9.2. Building a Celsius-Fahrenheit Converter

9.2.1. Goals

In this project, we will create a program that allows the user to convert temperatures between Celsius and Fahrenheit using Python. The user will be able to enter a temperature in one scale and see the equivalent temperature in the other scale. This project is a great opportunity to practice using basic arithmetic operations and implementing a simple user interface in Python.

Note: If you feel confident in your understanding and skills, try writing the project on your own. The following chapter will provide detailed instructions that you can refer to if needed.

9.2.2. Instructions

Below are the instructions but you can think about something different:

1. Start a new Python file in your text editor.
2. Define a function named **convert_temperature** that takes a single argument, **temp**, which represents the temperature to be converted.
3. Inside the function, use an if statement to check if the **temp** argument is in Celsius or Fahrenheit.
4. If the temp argument is in Celsius, convert it to Fahrenheit using the following formula: **F = (9/5) * C + 32**.
5. If the **temp** argument is in Fahrenheit, convert it to Celsius using the following formula: **C = (5/9) * (F - 32)**.
6. Return the converted temperature.
7. Outside the function, ask the user to enter a temperature and the scale it is in (Celsius or Fahrenheit).
8. Call the **convert_temperature** function with the user's input as the argument.
9. Print the return value of the **convert_temperature** function.

Note: If you feel confident in your skills, try writing the project on your own. The following chapter will provide a solution that you can use as a reference if needed.

9.2.3. Source code

Here is one possible solution among others that may exist:

The code defines a function named **convert_temperature** that takes a single argument, **temp**, which represents the temperature to be converted.

The function checks if the **temp** argument is in Celsius or Fahrenheit by checking the last character of the string:

- If the last character is "C", the function converts the temperature to Fahrenheit using the formula **F = (9/5) * C + 32**.
- If the last character is "F", the function converts the temperature to Celsius using the formula **C = (5/9) * (F - 32)**.

The main program gets the temperature and scale from the user and calls the **convert_temperature** function with the user's input as the argument. The program then prints the converted temperature.

```python
def convert_temperature(temp):
    # Check if the temperature is in Celsius or Fahrenheit
    if temp.endswith("C"):
        # Convert Celsius to Fahrenheit
        temp_f = (9/5) * float(temp[:-1]) + 32
        return "{:.1f}F".format(temp_f)
    elif temp.endswith("F"):
        # Convert Fahrenheit to Celsius
        temp_c = (5/9) * (float(temp[:-1]) - 32)
        return "{:.1f}C".format(temp_c)

# Get the temperature and scale from the user
temp = input("Enter a temperature and scale (e.g. 32C or 75F): ")

# Convert and print the temperature
converted_temp = convert_temperature(temp)
print("Converted temperature:", converted_temp)
```

9.2.4. Demonstration

Below are two examples of conversions (our inputs are in red):

```
$ python3 convert_temperature.py
Enter a temperature and scale (e.g. 32C or 75F): 35C
Converted temperature: 95.0F
```

```
$ python3 convert_temperature.py
Enter a temperature and scale (e.g. 32C or 75F): 95F
Converted temperature: 35.0C
```

9.3. Building a simple Calculator

9.3.1. Goals

In this project, we will create a simple calculator program using Python. The calculator will allow the user to perform basic math operations, including addition, subtraction, multiplication, and division. The user will be able to enter two numbers, choose an operation, and see the result. This project is a great opportunity to practice using basic arithmetic operators and functions in Python, as well as implementing a simple user interface.

The simple calculator program will work as below:

1. Run the calculator program.
2. Enter the first number that you want to use in your calculation.
3. Enter the second number that you want to use in your calculation.
4. Choose the operation that you want to perform:
    o Press 1 for addition.
    o Press 2 for subtraction.
    o Press 3 for multiplication.
    o Press 4 for division.
5. The program will display the result of the calculation.
6. To perform another calculation, press 1. To exit the program, press 2.

Note: If you feel confident in your understanding and skills, try writing the project on your own. The following chapter will provide detailed instructions that you can refer to if needed.

9.3.2.   Instructions

Here are the steps to build a basic calculator in Python:

1. Start a new Python file in your text editor.
2. Define a function named calculator that takes two arguments, **num1** and **num2**.
3. Inside the function, define a variable named **operation** and set it equal to an input statement that asks the user to choose an operation.
4. Create an if statement that checks if the user entered 1 for addition. If the user entered 1, the function should return the sum of **num1** and **num2**.
5. Create an elif statement that checks if the user entered 2 for subtraction. If the user entered 2, the function should return the difference between **num1** and **num2**.
6. Create another elif statement that checks if the user entered 3 for multiplication. If the user entered 3, the function should return the product of **num1** and **num2**.
7. Create another elif statement that checks if the user entered 4 for division. If the user entered 4, the function should return the quotient of **num1** and **num2**.
8. If the user entered any other value, print an error message.
9. Outside the function, define a variable named **result** and set it equal to the return value of the calculator function when called with two numbers as arguments.
10. Print the value of the **result**.
11. Create a loop that allows the user to continue performing calculations or exit the program.

Alternative:

- Instead of building a command-line interface using the Python input function, or you could create a graphical user interface using a library like PyQt or Tkinter.
- If you are building a graphical user interface, you will also need to design the layout and appearance of your calculator using widgets and layout managers.

Note: If you feel confident in your skills, try writing the project on your own. The following chapter will provide a solution that you can use as a reference if needed.

9.3.3. Source code

Here is one possible solution among others that may exist:

The code defines a function named **calculator** that takes two numbers as arguments and performs an operation chosen by the user. The function returns the result of the operation, or **None** if the user entered an invalid operation.

The main program loop allows the user to enter two numbers and perform a calculation, then asks if they want to perform another calculation. If the user enters "n", the program exits.

```python
# Define the calculator function
def calculator(num1, num2):
    # Ask the user to choose an operation
    operation = input("Choose an operation (1: addition, 2: subtraction,
3: multiplication, 4: division): ")

    # Perform the chosen operation
    if operation == "1":
        # Addition
        result = num1 + num2
    elif operation == "2":
        # Subtraction
        result = num1 - num2
    elif operation == "3":
        # Multiplication
        result = num1 * num2
    elif operation == "4":
        # Division
        result = num1 / num2
    else:
        # Invalid operation
        print("Invalid operation")
        result = None
    return result

# Main program loop
while True:
    # Get the numbers from the user
    num1 = float(input("Enter the first number: "))
    num2 = float(input("Enter the second number: "))
```

```
# Call the calculator function and print the result
result = calculator(num1, num2)
if result is not None:
  print("Result:", result)

# Ask the user if they want to perform another calculation
again = input("Perform another calculation? (y/n) ")
if again.lower() != "y":
  break
```

9.3.4. Demonstration

Below is an example of a calculation (our inputs are in red):

```
$ python3 calculator.py
Enter the first number: 1
Enter the second number: 3
Choose an operation (1: addition, 2: subtraction, 3: multiplication, 4:
division): 1
Result: 4.0
Perform another calculation? (y/n) y
Enter the first number: 2
Enter the second number: 1
Choose an operation (1: addition, 2: subtraction, 3: multiplication, 4:
division): 2
Result: 1.0
Perform another calculation? (y/n)
```

9.4. Building a simple Game

9.4.1. Goals

In this project, we will create a simple guessing game using Python. The game will generate a random number between a specified range, and the user will have to guess the number. The program will give feedback to the user, indicating whether their guess is too high or too low. The user will have a limited number of guesses, and the game will end when they either guess the correct number or run out of guesses. This project is a great opportunity to practice using Python's **random** module and implementing a simple looping structure.

Note: If you feel confident in your understanding and skills, try writing the project on your own. The following chapter will provide detailed instructions that you can refer to if needed.

9.4.2. Instructions

Below are the instructions but you can think about something different:

1. Start a new Python file in your text editor.
2. Import the **random** module.
3. Define a function named **guessing_game** that takes a single argument, **max_number**.
4. Inside the function, generate a random number between 1 and **max_number** and assign it to a variable named **secret_number**.
5. Define a variable named **attempts** and set it equal to 0. This variable will keep track of the number of guesses the user has made.
6. Create a loop that will run until the user either guesses the correct number or runs out of attempts.
7. Inside the loop, ask the user to enter a guess.
8. Increment the **attempts** variable by 1.
9. If the user's guess is equal to the **secret_number**, print a message indicating that they have won and exit the loop.
10. If the user's guess is less than the **secret_number**, print a message indicating that their guess is too low.
11. If the user's guess is greater than the **secret_number**, print a message indicating that their guess is too high.
12. If the user runs out of attempts, print a message indicating that they have lost and exit the loop.
13. Outside the function, call the **guessing_game** function with a number as an argument to specify the range of the secret number.

Note: If you feel confident in your skills, try writing the project on your own. The following chapter will provide a solution that you can use as a reference if needed.

9.4.3. Source code

Here is one possible solution among others that may exist:

The code defines a function named **guessing_game** that takes a single argument, **max_number**, which specifies the range of the secret number. The function generates a random number between 1 and **max_number** and assigns it to a variable named **secret_number**.

The function then enters a loop in which it prompts the user to enter a guess and checks if the guess is correct. If the guess is correct, the function prints a message indicating that the user has won and exits the loop. If the guess is too low or too high, the function prints a message indicating this and continues the loop.

If the user runs out of attempts, the function prints a message indicating that the user has lost and exits the loop.

```python
import random

def guessing_game(max_number):
    # Specify the maximum number of attempts
    max_attempts = 5

    # Generate a random number between 1 and max_number
    secret_number = random.randint(1, max_number)

    # Initialize the number of attempts
    attempts = 0

    # Start the guessing loop
    while True:
        # Ask the user to enter a guess
        guess = int(input("Enter your guess: "))

        # Increment the number of attempts
        attempts += 1

        # Check if the guess is correct
        if guess == secret_number:
            print("You win! You guessed the correct number in", attempts,
"attempts.")
            break
        elif guess < secret_number:
            print("Your guess is too low.")
        else:
            print("Your guess is too high.")

        # Check if the user has run out of attempts
        if attempts >= max_attempts:
            print("You lose! The correct number was", secret_number)
            break

# Main program
def main():
    # Specify the maximum number for the secret number
    max_number = 100
    guessing_game(max_number)

# Run the main program
if __name__ == "__main__":
    main()
```

9.4.4.   Demonstration

Below is an example of a game session (our inputs are in red):

```
$ python3 guessing_game.py
Enter your guess: 55
Your guess is too high.
Enter your guess: 33
Your guess is too low.
Enter your guess: 44
You win! You guessed the correct number in 3 attempts.
```

9.5. Building a Password Generator

9.5.1. Goals

In this project, we will create a program that generates random passwords using Python. The user will be able to specify the length of the password and whether they want it to include letters, numbers, and/or special characters. We will use Python's **random** module to generate the passwords. This project is a great opportunity to practice using string formatting and generating random values in Python.

Note: If you feel confident in your understanding and skills, try writing the project on your own. The following chapter will provide detailed instructions that you can refer to if needed.

9.5.2. Instructions

Below are the instructions but you can think about something different:

1. Start a new Python file in your text editor.
2. Import the **random** and **string** modules.
3. Define a function named **generate_password** that takes two arguments: **length** and **characters**.
4. Inside the function, define a variable named password and set it equal to an empty string. This variable will be used to store the generated password.
5. Create a loop that will run for the specified length of the password. Inside the loop, generate a random character using the **random** and **string** modules.
   - If the **characters** argument is "letters", generate a random lowercase or uppercase letter.
   - If the **characters** argument is "numbers", generate a random digit.
   - If the **characters** argument is "special", generate a random special character.
   - If the **characters** argument is "all", generate a random letter, digit, or special character.
6. Add the random character to the **password** string.
7. Return the **password** string when the loop has finished running.

8. Outside the function, ask the user for the desired length and character set for the password, and call the **generate_password** function with these values as arguments.
9. Print the return value of the **generate_password** function.

<u>Note</u>: If you feel confident in your skills, try writing the project on your own. The following chapter will provide a solution that you can use as a reference if needed.

9.5.3. Source code

Here is one possible solution among others that may exist :

This code defines a function named **generate_password** that takes two arguments:
- **length**, which specifies the number of characters in the password
- **characters**, which specifies the type of characters to include in the password

The function generates a random character based on the specified **characters** argument and adds it to the **password** string. The loop runs for the specified **length** of the password, generating the specified number of characters.

The main program gets the desired password length and character set from the user and calls the **generate_password** function with these values as arguments. The program then prints the generated password.

```python
import random
import string

def generate_password(length, characters):
    # Initialize an empty password string
    password = ""

    # Generate the specified number of characters
    for i in range(length):
        # Choose a random character type
        if characters == "letters":
            # Generate a random letter
            char = random.choice(string.ascii_letters)
        elif characters == "numbers":
            # Generate a random digit
            char = random.choice(string.digits)
        elif characters == "special":
            # Generate a random special character
            char = random.choice(string.punctuation)
        elif characters == "all":
            # Generate a random letter, digit, or special character
            char = random.choice(string.ascii_letters + string.digits +
string.punctuation)

        # Add the character to the password
        password += char
```

```
    # Return the password
    return password

# Get the desired password length and character set from the user
length = int(input("Enter the desired password length: "))
characters = input("Enter the desired character set (letters, numbers,
special, all): ")

# Generate and print the password
password = generate_password(length, characters)
print("Generated password:", password)
```

9.5.4. Demonstration

Below are examples of a use (our inputs are in red):

```
$ python3 password_generator.py
Enter the desired password length: 10
Enter the desired character set (letters, numbers, special, all): all
Generated password: _9D5c1Ym{?
```

```
$ python3 password_generator.py
Enter the desired password length: 8
Enter the desired character set (letters, numbers, special, all):
letters
Generated password: oxLMXWjt
```

9.6. Building a TO-DO List

9.6.1. Goals

In this project, we will create a program that allows the user to manage a **to-do list** using
Python. The program will provide several options for the user to choose from, including
adding a new task to the list, removing a task from the list, and viewing the current tasks on
the list. The program will store the tasks in a list data structure and allow the user to perform
various operations on the list.

This project is a great opportunity to practice using lists, implementing basic user input and
output, and creating a simple user interface in Python.

Note: If you feel confident in your understanding and skills, try writing the project on your
own. The following chapter will provide detailed instructions that you can refer to if needed.

9.6.2. Instructions

Below are the instructions but you can think about something different:

1. Start a new Python file in your text editor.
2. Define a list named **tasks** that will store the to-do list tasks.
3. Define a function named **view_tasks** that takes a single argument, **tasks**.
4. Inside the function, use a for loop to iterate over the **tasks** list and print each task.
5. Define a function named **add_task** that takes a single argument, **tasks**.
6. Inside the function, ask the user to enter a new task and append it to the **tasks** list.
7. Define a function named **remove_task** that takes a single argument, **tasks**.
8. Inside the function, ask the user to enter the task they want to remove and use the remove method to remove it from the **tasks** list.
9. Inside a **while** loop, present the user with a list of options (view tasks, add task, remove task, quit) and ask them to choose an option.
10. Use if statements to call the appropriate function based on the user's choice.
11. When the user chooses to quit, exit the while loop and end the program.

Note: If you feel confident in your skills, try writing the project on your own. The following chapter will provide a solution that you can use as a reference if needed.

9.6.3. Source code

Here is one possible solution among others that may exist :

The code creates a new empty list named **tasks**. This list will be used to store the tasks that the user wants to add to their to-do list. The list is initialized as an empty list, meaning that it does not contain any elements at the start of the program.

The user will be able to add tasks to the list using the **add_task** function, and view the current tasks using the **view_tasks** function.

The user can also remove tasks from the list using the **remove_task** function. The **tasks** list will be passed as an argument to these functions whenever they are called, allowing the functions to access and manipulate the list as needed.

```python
# Define the to-do list tasks
tasks = []

def view_tasks(tasks):
  # Print the current tasks
  if tasks:
    print("Current tasks:")
    for i, task in enumerate(tasks):
      print(i+1, task)
```

```python
    else:
        print("No tasks to display.")

def add_task(tasks):
    # Ask the user for a new task and add it to the list
    new_task = input("Enter a new task: ")
    tasks.append(new_task)
    print("Task added to list.")

def remove_task(tasks):
    # Ask the user for the task to remove and remove it from the list
    task_to_remove = int(input("Enter the task to remove: "))
    tasks.pop(task_to_remove - 1)
    print("Task removed from list.")

# Present the user with a list of options
while True:
    print("""
To-do List Options:
1. View tasks
2. Add task
3. Remove task
4. Quit
""")
    choice = input("Enter your choice: ")

    # Choose the appropriate action
    if choice == "1":
        view_tasks(tasks)
    elif choice == "2":
        add_task(tasks)
    elif choice == "3":
        remove_task(tasks)
    elif choice == "4":
        break
    else:
        print("Invalid choice. Try again.")
```

9.6.4. Demonstration

Below is an example of use (our inputs are in red):

```
$ python3 todo_list.py

To-do List Options:
1. View tasks
2. Add task
3. Remove task
4. Quit

Enter your choice: 2
Enter a new task: Learn C
Task added to list.
```

73

```
    To-do List Options:
    1. View tasks
    2. Add task
    3. Remove task
    4. Quit

Enter your choice: 2
Enter a new task: Learn Python
Task added to list.

    To-do List Options:
    1. View tasks
    2. Add task
    3. Remove task
    4. Quit

Enter your choice: 1
Current tasks:
1 Learn C
2 Learn Python

    To-do List Options:
    1. View tasks
    2. Add task
    3. Remove task
    4. Quit

Enter your choice: 3
Enter the task to remove: 1
Task removed from list.

    To-do List Options:
    1. View tasks
    2. Add task
    3. Remove task
    4. Quit

Enter your choice: 1
Current tasks:
1 Learn Python

    To-do List Options:
    1. View tasks
    2. Add task
    3. Remove task
    4. Quit

Enter your choice: 4
```

In this example:
- We add two tasks ("Learn C" and then "Learn Python")
- Then we delete the first task "Learn C" using its index
- Then we list the tasks to verify that we only have one remaining task: "Learn Python"
- Finally, we exit the program.

9.7. Building a Web Scraper

9.7.1. Goals

"In this project, we will create a program that builds a web scraper using Python. The web scraper will be able to retrieve and extract data from a specific website or web page. The user will be able to specify the target website and the specific data they want to extract from the website. This project is a great opportunity to practice using Python's **requests** and **BeautifulSoup** libraries, as well as implementing basic web scraping techniques.

> **BeautifulSoup** is a Python library that is used for web scraping and parsing HTML and XML content. It allows you to easily extract data from a website or web page by searching for specific HTML elements and attributes. **BeautifulSoup** makes it easy to extract data from websites and is a powerful tool for web scraping projects in Python. It is fast, flexible, and easy to use, making it a popular choice among developers.

Note: If you feel confident in your understanding and skills, try writing the project on your own. The following chapter will provide detailed instructions that you can refer to if needed.

9.7.2. Instructions

Below are the instructions but you can think about something different:

- Start a new Python file in your text editor.
- Import the **requests** and **BeautifulSoup** libraries.
- Define a function named **scrape** that takes two arguments:
  - **url**, which represents the target website
  - **data**, which represents the specific data to be extracted
- Inside the function, use the **requests** library to send a GET request to the target **url**.
- Use the **BeautifulSoup** library to parse the HTML content of the website.
- Use the **find** or **find_all** method to locate the specific data to be extracted.
- Extract the data and return it.
- Outside the function, ask the user to enter the target website and the specific data they want to extract.
- Call the **scrape** function with the user's input as the arguments.
- Print the return value of the **scrape** function.

> To install BeautifulSoup, you can use **pip**, the Python package manager.
>
> Open a terminal and run the following command:
>
> `pip install beautifulsoup4`

This will install the latest version of BeautifulSoup for you.

Alternatively, you can also install BeautifulSoup using **conda**, the package manager for the Anaconda distribution of Python. To do this, run the following command in a terminal:

```
conda install -c anaconda beautifulsoup4
```

Once the installation is complete, you can import BeautifulSoup in your Python code using the following line:

```
from bs4 import BeautifulSoup
```

Note: If you feel confident in your skills, try writing the project on your own. The following chapter will provide a solution that you can use as a reference if needed.

9.7.3. Source code

Here is one possible solution among others that may exist.

The user will need to provide the following input:

- Target website: This is the URL of the website that the user wants to scrape.
- Specific data to extract: This is the specific data that the user wants to extract from the website. This should be a valid HTML element, such as a div, span, or p tag.

The code imports the **requests** and **BeautifulSoup** libraries and defines a function named **scrape** that takes two arguments: **url**, which represents the target website, and **data**, which represents the specific data to be extracted.

The function uses the **requests** library to send a GET request to the target **url** and the **BeautifulSoup** library to parse the HTML content of the website. It then uses the **find** method to locate the specific data to be extracted and returns it.

The main program gets the target website and specific data from the user and calls the **scrape** function with these values as arguments. The program then prints the extracted data.

```python
import requests
from bs4 import BeautifulSoup

def scrape(url, data):
    # Send a GET request to the target website
    response = requests.get(url)

    # Parse the HTML content of the website
    soup = BeautifulSoup(response.content, "html.parser")
```

```
    # Locate the specific data to be extracted
    extracted_data = soup.find(data)

    # Return the extracted data
    return extracted_data

# Get the target website and specific data from the user
url = input("Enter the target website: ")
data = input("Enter the specific data to extract: ")

# Scrape and print the data
scraped_data = scrape(url, data)
print("Extracted data:", scraped_data)
```

9.7.4. Demonstration

Below is an example of use (our inputs are in red):

```
$ python3 web_scraper.py
Enter the target website: http://www.talenceinstitute.com
Enter the specific data to extract: p
Extracted data: <p>We have more than 15 years in Cyber Security and
teaching.</p>
```

9.8. Building a Tic-Tac-Toe Game

9.8.1. Goals

In this project, we will create a program that generates a simple tic-tac-toe game using Python.

The game will be played on a **3x3 grid** and will allow the user to play against the computer. The user will be able to choose whether they want to play as X or O, and the computer will automatically choose the other symbol.

The game will continue until one player gets three of their symbols in a row (horizontally, vertically, or diagonally) or until the grid is filled with no winner. This project is a great opportunity to practice using lists and implementing basic game logic in Python.

Note: If you feel confident in your understanding and skills, try writing the project on your own. The following chapter will provide detailed instructions that you can refer to if needed.

9.8.2. Instructions

Below are the instructions but you can think about something different:

1. Start a new Python file in your text editor.
2. Begin by defining the game grid as a list of lists, with each inner list representing a row of the grid and each element within the inner list representing a column. Initialize the grid to be a 3x3 grid of empty spaces represented by the string " ".
3. Define a function **display_grid(grid)** that takes in a grid and prints the current game grid. The function should iterate through each row in the grid and print it.
4. Define a function **get_move(grid, player)** that takes in a grid and a player symbol (either "X" or "O"). The function should ask the user for their move and update the grid with the player symbol. The function should continue to ask for the user's move until they provide a valid move (an empty space on the grid).
5. Define a function **check_win(grid)** that takes in a grid and checks if there are three of the same symbols in a row (horizontally, vertically, or diagonally). If there are three of the same symbols in a row, the function should return True. If the grid is filled with no winner, the function should return None. Otherwise, the function should return False.
6. Ask the user which symbol they want to play as, either "X" or "O".
7. Determine who goes first by randomly selecting either "X" or "O" using the **random** module. Set the computer's symbol to the symbol that was not selected and set the other player's symbol to the symbol that was selected.
8. Start the game by entering a loop that will continue until the game is over. Inside the loop, call the **display_grid()** function to display the current game grid.
9. It is now the user's turn. Call the **get_move()** function to allow the user to make their move.
10. Check if the user won by calling the **check_win()** function and passing in the grid. If the function returns True, display the grid and print "You win!" then break out of the loop. If the function returns None, display the grid and print "It's a draw!" then break out of the loop.
11. It is now the computer's turn. Select a random empty space on the grid and update the grid with the computer's symbol.
12. Check if the computer won by calling the **check_win()** function and passing in the grid. If the function returns True, display the grid and print "The computer wins!" then break out of the loop. If the function returns None, display the grid and print "It's a draw!" then break out of the loop.

Note: If you feel confident in your skills, try writing the project on your own. The following chapter will provide a solution that you can use as a reference if needed.

9.8.3. Source code

Here is one possible solution among others that may exist :

```python
# Define the game grid
grid = [[" "," "," "],[" "," "," "],[" "," "," "]]

def display_grid(grid):
  # Print the current game grid
  for row in grid:
    print(row)

def get_move(grid, player):
  # Ask the user for their move and update the grid
  while True:
    move = input(f"{player}, enter your move (row column): ")
    row, col = move.split()
    row, col = int(row), int(col)
    if grid[row][col] == " ":
      grid[row][col] = player
      break
    else:
      print("Invalid move. Try again.")

def check_win(grid):
  # Check if there are three of the same symbols in a row (horizontally,
vertically, or diagonally)
  for row in range(3):
    if grid[row][0] == grid[row][1] == grid[row][2] and grid[row][0] !=
" ":
      return True
  for col in range(3):
    if grid[0][col] == grid[1][col] == grid[2][col] and grid[0][col] !=
" ":
      return True
  if grid[0][0] == grid[1][1] == grid[2][2] and grid[0][0] != " ":
    return True
  if grid[0][2] == grid[1][1] == grid[2][0] and grid[0][2] != " ":
    return True
  # Check if the grid is filled with no winner
  for row in grid:
    if " " in row:
      return False
  return None

# Ask the user which symbol they want to play as
player = input("Do you want to be X or O? ")

# Determine who goes first
import random
if random.randint(0, 1) == 0:
  computer = "O"
else:
  computer = "X"
if player == "X":
  other = "O"
else:
  other = "X"

# Start the game
while True:
  # Display the grid
```

```
display_grid(grid)

# User's turn
get_move(grid, player)

# Check if the user won
result = check_win(grid)
if result == True:
  display_grid(grid)
  print("You win!")
  break
elif result == None:
  display_grid(grid)
  print("It's a draw!")
  break

# Computer's turn
while True:
  row = random.randint(0, 2)
  col = random.randint(0, 2)
  if grid[row][col] == " ":
    grid[row][col] = computer
    break

# Check if the computer won
result = check_win(grid)
if result == True:
  display_grid(grid)
  print("The computer wins!")
  break
elif result == None:
  display_grid(grid)
  print("It's a draw!")
  break
```

Reminder on Element Count: In Python, it is important to remember that the element count in a list starts at 0, rather than 1. This means that the first element in a list is at index 0, the second element is at index 1, and so on. For example, in the list [1, 2, 3, 4], the first element is 1 and is at index 0, the second element is 2 and is at index 1, and so on.

This can be confusing for beginners, as many other programming languages start the element count at 1. Make sure to keep this in mind when working with lists in Python.

9.8.4. Demonstration

Below is an example of a game session. In this example, we chose to play as "X" and made three moves to win. Our inputs to the game are highlighted in red.

```
$ python3 tic-tac-toe.py
Do you want to be X or O? X
[' ', ' ', ' ']
[' ', ' ', ' ']
[' ', ' ', ' ']
```

```
X, enter your move (row column): 1 1
[' ', ' ', ' ']
[' ', 'X', ' ']
[' ', ' ', 'O']
X, enter your move (row column): 0 2
['O', ' ', 'X']
[' ', 'X', ' ']
[' ', ' ', 'O']
X, enter your move (row column): 2 0
['O', ' ', 'X']
[' ', 'X', ' ']
['X', ' ', 'O']
You win!
```

It's important to note that the computer's moves are made randomly, so it is relatively easy to beat. There is no intelligence programmed into the computer's moves.

9.9. Building a Weather Forecast App (API)

9.9.1. Goals

In this project, you will build a simple command-line app that retrieves and displays weather forecast data for a given location. You will use the OpenWeatherMap API to retrieve the data, and the requests library to send API requests and process the responses.

Note: If you feel confident in your understanding and skills, try writing the project on your own. The following chapter will provide detailed instructions that you can refer to if needed.

9.9.2. Instructions

Below are the instructions but you can think about something different:

1. Import the necessary libraries (e.g. **requests**).
2. Define a function to retrieve the latitude and longitude for a given location using the OpenWeatherMap API. This function should send a request to the API with the specified location and API key, and return the response as a dictionary.
3. Define a function to retrieve weather data from the OpenWeatherMap API using the latitude and longitude of a given location. This function should send a request to the API with the specified coordinates and API key, and return the response as a dictionary.
4. Define a function to parse the weather data into a usable format. This function should extract the relevant data (e.g. temperature, humidity, wind speed, weather description) from the weather data dictionary and return it as a new dictionary.

5. Define a function to display the forecast to the user. This function should print out the forecast data in a user-friendly format.
6. In the main program, prompt the user for their location and API key. Use these to retrieve the weather data for the location and parse it into a usable format. Then display the forecast to the user.
7. Test the program to ensure it is working as expected.

Note: If you feel confident in your skills, try writing the project on your own. The following chapter will provide a solution that you can use as a reference if needed.

9.9.3. Source code

Here is one possible solution among others that may exist :

The program uses the OpenWeatherMap API to retrieve and display the current weather forecast for a given location, with the ability to accept a city name as the location.

The program is composed of four functions:

- **get_coordinates**: retrieves the latitude and longitude for a given location using the OpenWeatherMap API
- **get_weather_data**: retrieves weather data from the OpenWeatherMap API using the latitude and longitude of the location
- **parse_weather_data**: parses the weather data into a usable format
- **display_forecast**: displays the forecast data to the user

The main program prompts the user for their location and OpenWeatherMap API key, retrieves and parses the weather data for the location, and displays the forecast data to the user.

```python
import requests

# Function to retrieve the latitude and longitude for a given location
using the OpenWeatherMap API
def get_coordinates(location, api_key):
    # Construct the API request URL
    api_url =
f"https://api.openweathermap.org/geo/1.0/direct?q={location}&limit=1&app
id={api_key}"

    # Send the request to the API and retrieve the response
    response = requests.get(api_url)

    # Check the status code of the response
    if response.status_code == 404:
        # Return an empty dictionary if the location is not found
        return {}
    else:
        # Return the first element of the list of dictionaries as a
```

```python
dictionary
        return response.json()[0]

# Function to retrieve weather data from the OpenWeatherMap API
def get_weather_data(location, api_key):
    # Retrieve the latitude and longitude for the location
    coordinates = get_coordinates(location, api_key)

    # Check if the location was found
    if coordinates:
        # Extract the latitude and longitude from the response
        lat = coordinates["lat"]
        lon = coordinates["lon"]

        # Construct the API request URL
        api_url =
f"https://api.openweathermap.org/data/2.5/weather?lat={lat}&lon={lon}&ap
pid={api_key}"
        print("Latitude:", lat)
        print("Longitude:", lon)
        print("API URL:", api_url)

        # Send the request to the API and retrieve the response
        response = requests.get(api_url)

        # Return the response as a dictionary
        return response.json()
    else:
        # Return an empty dictionary if the location is not found
        return {}

# Function to parse the weather data into a usable format
def parse_weather_data(weather_data):
    # Extract the relevant data from the weather data dictionary
    forecast = {
        "temperature": weather_data["main"]["temp"],
        "humidity": weather_data["main"]["humidity"],
        "wind_speed": weather_data["wind"]["speed"],
        "description": weather_data["weather"][0]["description"]
    }

    # Return the forecast data
    return forecast

# Function to display the forecast to the user
def display_forecast(forecast):
    # Print out the forecast data
    print(f"Temperature: {forecast['temperature']} degrees Celsius")
    print(f"Humidity: {forecast['humidity']}%")
    print(f"Wind speed: {forecast['wind_speed']} m/s")
    print(f"Description: {forecast['description']}")

# Main program
def main():
    # Ask the user for their location and API key
    location = input("Enter your location (city name): ")
    api_key = input("Enter your OpenWeatherMap API key: ")

    # Retrieve the weather data for the location
```

```
    weather_data = get_weather_data(location, api_key)

    # Parse the weather data into a usable format
    forecast = parse_weather_data(weather_data)

    # Display the forecast to the user
    display_forecast(forecast)

# Run the main program
if __name__ == "__main__":
    main()
```

9.9.4. Demonstration

Below is an example of use (our inputs are in red):

```
$ python3 weather_forecast.py
Enter your location (city name): New-York City
Enter your OpenWeatherMap API key: API Key removed
Latitude: 40.7127281
Longitude: -74.0060152
API URL:
https://api.openweathermap.org/data/2.5/weather?lat=40.7127281&lon=-74.0
060152&appid=<removed api key>
Temperature: 274.77 degrees Celsius
Humidity: 61%
Wind speed: 2.06 m/s
Description: clear sky
```

<u>Note</u>: The temperature values returned by the server may be incorrect. However, the coordinates used in the API request are correct (this can be verified by examining the API request URL.

Chapter 10: Conclusion

10.1. Recap of key Python concepts

In this book, we have covered a wide range of Python concepts and techniques. In this final chapter, we will summarize some of the key concepts that you have learned:

- Python is a high-level, interpreted programming language that is widely used for web development, scientific computing, data analysis, and more.
- Variables are used to store and manipulate data in Python. There are several different types of variables, including strings, booleans, and numbers.
- Operators allow you to perform operations on variables, such as assignment, comparison, and arithmetic.
- Data types are used to store and organize data in Python. Some common data types include lists, tuples, and dictionaries.
- Control structures, such as if/elif/else statements, for loops, and while loops, allow you to control the flow of your code.
- Functions are reusable blocks of code that can be called with different arguments. Functions can have parameters and return values.
- Modules and libraries are collections of pre-written Python code that you can use in your own programs.
- Python provides a wide range of built-in functions and methods that can be used to perform common tasks, such as formatting strings, converting data types, and working with lists and dictionaries.

We hope that this book has helped you to get started with Python and provided you with a solid foundation to build upon. Thank you for reading, and we hope that you continue to learn and grow as a Python developer.

10.2. Next steps for learning Python

Now that you have completed this book, you have a **solid foundation** in Python programming. Here are some next steps that you can take to continue learning and improving your skills:

- **Stay up-to-date** with the latest developments in Python. The Python community is constantly improving and updating the language, and it's important to stay aware of these changes.

- **Practice** writing code on your own: The best way to get better at programming is to practice writing code. Try to come up with your own problems to solve and write programs to solve them.
- **Work on a real-world project**: Look for a project that you can work on that will use the skills you have learned in this book. This can be a great way to apply your knowledge and learn new skills at the same time.
- **Join online communities**: There are many online communities dedicated to Python programming where you can ask questions, get help with problems, and share your projects with others. Some examples include Stack Overflow, Reddit's r/learnprogramming, and the Python forums.
- **Learn more advanced concepts**: There is always more to learn in programming. Consider learning about more advanced topics such as data structures, algorithms, and machine learning.

We are working on a second Python book that will cover advanced concepts and guide readers to the expert level. This book will be a continuation of the current one. Please keep an eye out for updates.

Congratulations on completing this book! We hope that you have gained a strong understanding of Python programming and are ready to take your skills to the next level.

www.ingramcontent.com/pod-product-compliance
Lightning Source LLC
LaVergne TN
LVHW051643050326
832903LV00022B/871